Hi _____________ , shall we start our adventure to Arctic?

My name is Mika. I will be your tourist guide for this exciting arctic adventure.

We will learn about animals in the Arctic together.
The North Pole is in the middle of the Arctic Ocean
which is surrounded by the landmasses of North
America, Europe and Asia.

The poles of the planet are places
of extremely cold and dry. Make
sure you wear extremely warm cloth.

Let's take a rest first in Igloo. We will continue our exciting journey tomorrow.

This is

ARCTIC FOX

They can be found on any land north of
the Arctic Circle, across from Canada to
Russia, Europe, Greenland, and Iceland. ...

There are cute but extremely
well-adapted to the harsh, frigid
temperatures of the Arctic. They can
endure temperature as low as -70 Celcius

This is

ARCTIC HARE

There are the biggest species of hare, and has a thick white coat that conserves heat. They are herbivores, and eat the leaves of the various shrubs.

This is

REINDEER

They live in the Arctic tundra and damp forests of Greenland, Russia, Alaska, Scandinavia and Canada

They are the only deer species in which both the male *and* female can grow antlers and they can live up to 15 years.

This is

SNOWY OWL

This white owl adorable right? Don't mistake their cuteness. They are fantastic predator and quite large.

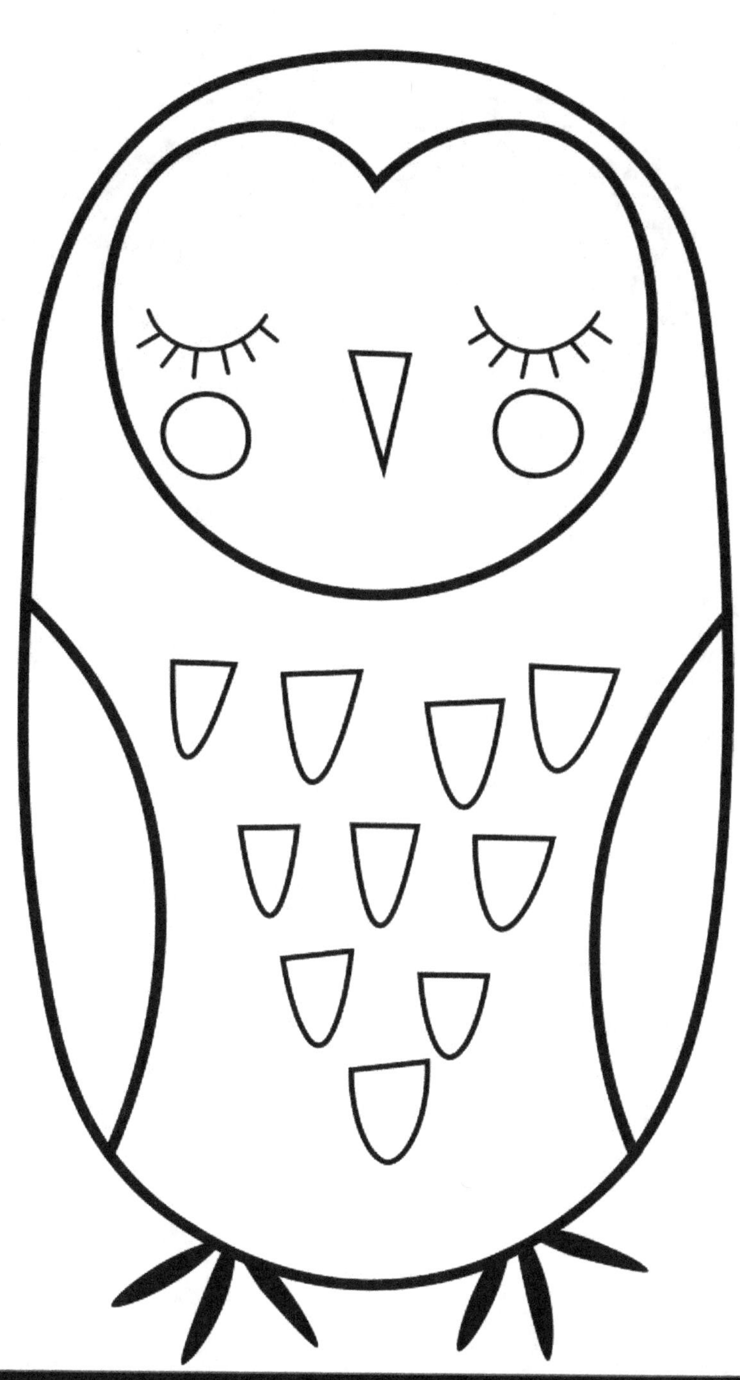

Unlike most of the owls that are hunting at night, they hunt during day and night.

This is

POLAR BEAR

They are the largest carnivores on Earth. They can measure over 2.5m long and weigh over 680 kg

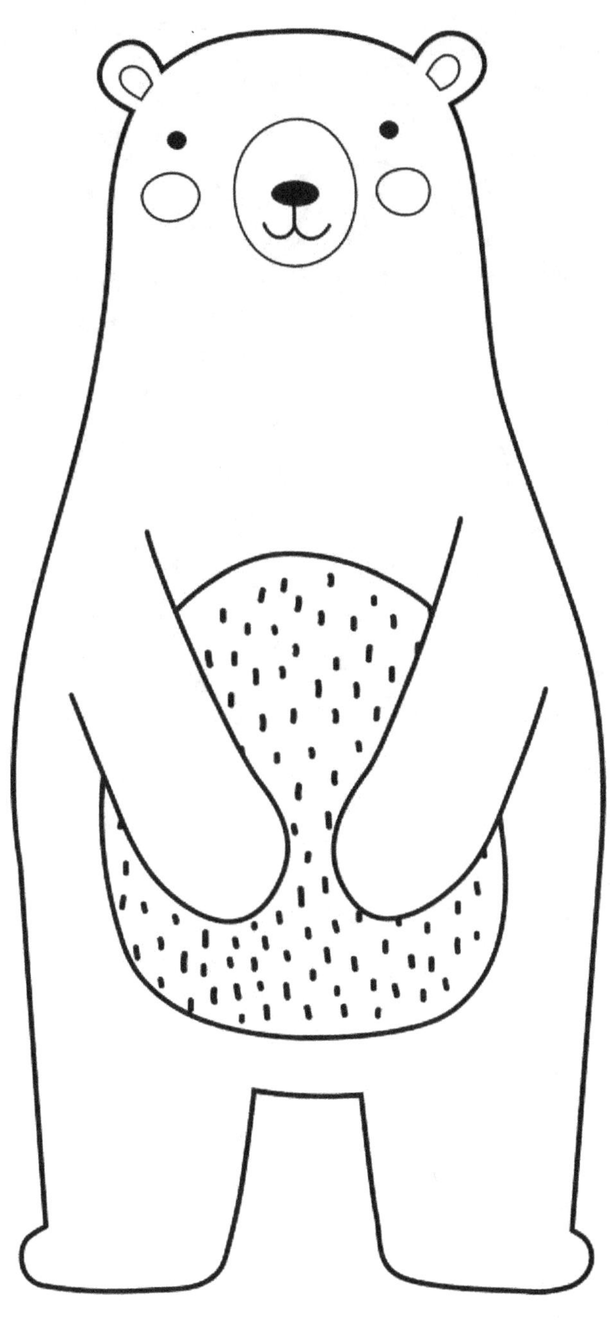

They eat mostly seals and can sniff
out prey from up to 16km away

This is

SEAL

Seals are semiaquatic marine mammals. They spend most of their time diving and swimming in the icy waters and can remain submerged up to 15 minutes.

Their average lifespan is about 20 years old and there are 33 species of Seals in the world.

This is

WALRUS

They are large marine mammals found near the
Arctic Circle and can weight up to 1.5 tons.
Their average life span is around 40 years old.

Both male and female have tusk.
Their tusk can grow up to 1 metre
and useful in many ways.

This is

ARCTIC WOLF

Arctic wolfs are smaller than grey wolfs and have smaller ear and shorter muzzles to retain their body heat in extremely cold temperature.

This is

NARWHAL

Narwhals are knowns as 'unicorns of the sea'
They have a tusk-like unicorn. Their tusk is
a tooth and can grow up to 10 feet long.

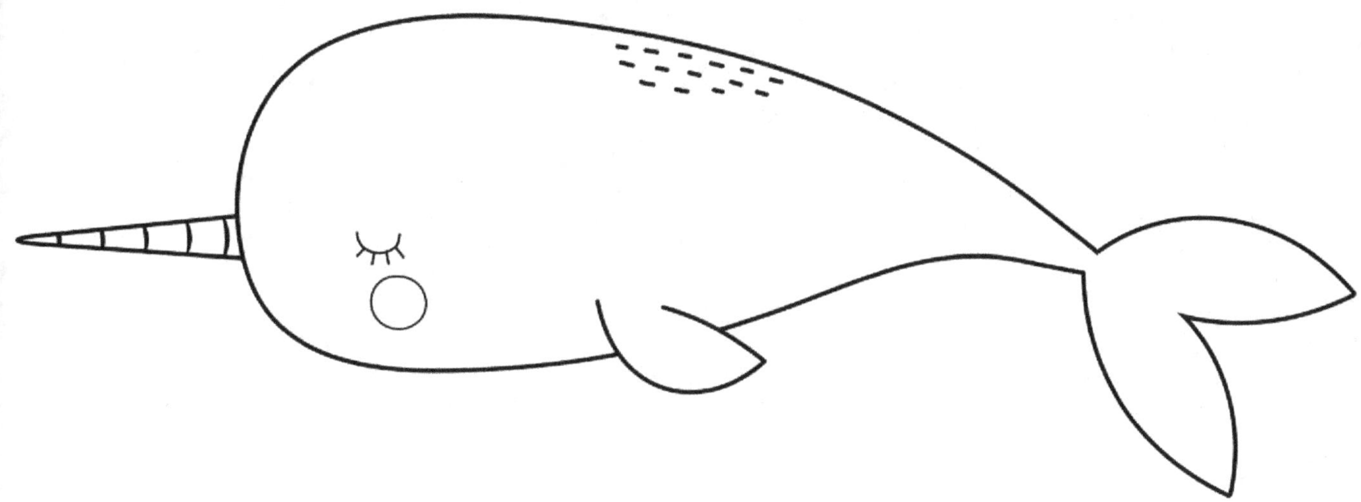

They have never been successfully kept in captivity, and you can only view them in the wild. They can live up to 50 years, and they change colour with age.